T0341633

"As a pastor, I get asked lots of questions. I'm approached by unbelievers seeking to understand the gospel, new believers unsure about next steps, and maturing believers wanting help answering questions from their Christian family, friends, neighbors, or coworkers. It's in these moments that I wish I had a book to give them that was brief, answered their questions, and pointed them in the right direction for further study. Church Questions is a series that provides just that. Each booklet tackles one question in a biblical, brief, and practical manner. The series may be called Church Questions, but it could be called 'Church Answers.' I intend to pick these up by the dozens and give them away regularly. You should too."

Juan R. Sanchez, Senior Pastor, High Pointe Baptist Church, Austin, Texas

"Where can we Christians find reliable answers to our common questions about life together at church—without having to plow through long, expensive books? The Church Questions booklets meet our need with answers that are biblical, thoughtful, and practical. For pastors, this series will prove a trustworthy resource for guiding church members toward deeper wisdom and stronger unity."

Ray Ortlund, President, Renewal Ministries

What
Is a
Church?

Church Questions

What
Is a
Church?

Matthew Emadi

WHEATON, ILLINOIS

What Is a Church?

© 2024 by 9Marks

Published by Crossway
        1300 Crescent Street
        Wheaton, Illinois 60187

Series design: Jordan Singer

First printing 2024

Printed in the United States of America

Trade paperback ISBN: 978-1-4335-9233-1
ePub ISBN: 978-1-4335-9235-5
PDF ISBN: 978-1-4335-9234-8

Library of Congress Cataloging-in-Publication Data

Names: Emadi, Matthew, 1984- author.
Title: What is a church? / Matt Emadi.
Description: Wheaton, Illinois : Crossway, [2023] | Series: Church questions | Includes bibliographical references and index.
Identifiers: LCCN 2023033741 (print) | LCCN 2023033742 (ebook) | ISBN 9781433592331 (trade paperback) | ISBN 9781433592348 (pdf) | ISBN 9781433592355 (epub)
Subjects: LCSH: Church.
Classification: LCC BV600.3 .E57 2023 (print) | LCC BV600.3 (ebook) | DDC 260—dc23/eng/20231204
LC record available at https://lccn.loc.gov/2023033741
LC ebook record available at https://lccn.loc.gov/2023033742

Crossway is a publishing ministry of Good News Publishers.

BP			33	32	31	30	29	28	27	26	25	24
15	14	13	12	11	10	9	8	7	6	5	4	3	2	1

To me, though I am the very least of all the saints, this grace was given, to preach to the Gentiles the unsearchable riches of Christ, and to bring to light for everyone what is the plan of the mystery hidden for ages in God, who created all things, so that through the church the manifold wisdom of God might now be made known to the rulers and authorities in the heavenly places.

Ephesians 3:8–10

I want you to listen to a conversation—one I have frequently with all sorts of folks. For the sake of this illustration, we'll call my dialogue partner "Lone Ranger." The conversation goes something like this:

Me: Hey, Lone Ranger, how are you? What church are you attending now?

Lone Ranger: Church? I don't really attend church. I have Christian friends that I get together with. I fellowship with them. That's basically my "church." My Christian friends.

Me: No, I don't think that is correct. The church isn't just a group of Christian friends hanging out. It's about—

Lone Ranger: Oh, come on! Jesus didn't set up an organized religion; he made disciples. The church is a people, and all Christians are part of the church. Wherever you have Christians, you have a church. We're a church right here—you and me—because we're two people who follow Jesus.

Me: No, we're not a church.

Lone Ranger: Yes, we are.

Me: No, we're not.

Lone Ranger: Yes, we are.

Me: No, we're not.

Lone Ranger: Yes, we are.

Me: Okay, we sound a bit ridiculous. Let me ask you a couple of questions. Do you believe the Bible is God's word and our ultimate authority?

Lone Ranger: Yes, I do.

Me: Do you believe that Jesus is our King and we must obey his commands?

Lone Ranger: Of course.

Me: Okay, how are we supposed to obey Jesus's commands in Matthew 18 without a local church? Jesus tells us how to care for a brother in unrepentant sin. He says if this brother refuses to repent, then we are to tell it to the "the church" (Matt. 18:17). Who is that?

Lone Ranger: What do you mean?

Me: Well, you and I both agree that Jesus gave us a command that he expects us to keep. He expects us to handle the kind of situation Matthew 18 describes by telling the sins of an unrepentant person to the church. So who is that? Who is the church? How do we identify this thing that Jesus calls the church so that we can fulfill his command?

Lone Ranger: Ummmm . . .

Me: Is it possible to "tell it" to the universal church?

Lone Ranger: Well . . . uh . . . I guess not.

Me: So from just this one text of Scripture, we can see that Jesus expects a church to consist of a group of people who gather together to make important decisions. The universal church simply cannot fulfill this command, neither can some Christians who occasionally bump into each other or casually get together once in a while. Jesus expects his followers to belong to a defined, organized, local body of believers called a "church" so that they can make some extremely important decisions.

Lone Ranger: Well . . . you know what . . . actually . . . I have to get going.

I have variations of this conversation so often that sometimes I feel like Bill Murray in *Groundhog Day*. For the record, I'm not complaining. One of my greatest joys as a pastor is to help people see what the Bible says about the church.

But why is this conversation so common?

Doesn't it seem strange that one of the most essential parts of the Christian life—the church—is also one of the most misunderstood or at least under-understood? Most Christians gather with their local churches every Sunday, if not more often. They serve their churches; they give their hard-earned money to support their churches; they regularly pray for their churches. But if we asked most Christians, "What is a church?" I bet they'd struggle to answer. Many of these same Christians can articulate the doctrine of the Trinity, justification by faith alone, and perhaps even their position on the millennium. But ask them to define "church," and they have a difficult time.

My hope is that by the time you finish this booklet, you will have a ready answer the next time someone asks you, "What is a church anyway?"

Universal Church or Local Church?

Lone Ranger, my fictitious conversation partner, was right about one thing: there is such a thing as the universal church. The universal church consists of all of God's people everywhere throughout history. God gathers every one of his people into the universal church under the lordship of Christ. Jesus is the "head" of the church (Eph. 1:22; 4:15; 5:23). His headship (authority) is not localized to one particular church. His headship is universal—over all believers at all times in all places.

Christians have confessed for centuries the words of the Nicene Creed: "And we believe that there is one holy, catholic and apostolic church." That word "catholic" doesn't mean Roman Catholic (with popes and priests and the mass and all of that). "Catholic" simply means universal. We could say more, but the universal church is a concept taught in the Bible and affirmed by historic Christian creeds.

But how do we identify the people who belong to the universal church? Who are they? Where are they?

Well, Scripture teaches that members of the universal church "show up" in local churches. They gather with God's people in real time and space. The local church is where the universal church becomes visible. In other words, our participation in the local church *demonstrates* that we belong to the universal church.

Imagine bumping into a 7'4" man playing pick-up basketball at the park. He's wearing an NBA basketball t-shirt and can shoot the lights out. Curiosity piqued, you ask him if he is an NBA player.

"Yes, I am," he says.

Your next question would probably be, "What team do you play for?"

"Team? Well, I am not currently playing or practicing with a team," he responds. "I told you I play in the National Basketball Association. I didn't say I play for a team."

So you inquire a bit further: "What teams have you played for?"

"None," he responds.

With a puzzled look on your face, you try to get more clarity. "So let me see if I understand? You say you are an NBA player, but you have no team, you don't practice, you don't play in games. You have not received a paycheck from the NBA, and no NBA team currently has you on their roster. Is that correct?"

"Yes," he says.

My hunch is that you would leave that conversation highly suspicious, if not convinced, that this man does not actually play in the NBA.

Should we feel the same way about someone who claims to be a Christian yet doesn't belong to a local church? Probably. Is it possible to be in the universal church but not part of a local church? Yes, it's possible. But local church membership makes universal church membership visible.

Defining "Church"

So what is a church? Jonathan Leeman and Colin Hansen have provided a clear and biblically faithful answer to that question in their book *Rediscover Church: Why the Body of Christ Is Essential.* I'll use their definition of the local church as our starting point. Here's what they say:

> A church is a group of Christians who assemble as an earthly embassy of Christ's heavenly kingdom to affirm one another as his citizens through the ordinances; to proclaim the good news and commands of Christ the King; and to display God's own holiness and love through a unified and diverse people in all the world, following the teaching and example of the elders.[1]

Perhaps that definition feels a bit overwhelming, but the rest of this booklet will unpack it bit by bit. Let's break the definition down into six parts. A local church is

1. a group of Christians
2. who assemble as an earthly embassy of Christ's heavenly kingdom
3. to affirm one another as his citizens through the ordinances;
4. to proclaim the good news and commands of Christ the King; and

5. to display God's own holiness and love through a unified and diverse people in all the world,

6. following the teaching and example of the elders.

1. A Group of Christians

If we're going to understand what a church is, then we need to understand what it means to be a Christian. Local churches would not exist without Christians, and Christians would not exist without God's gracious saving power.

John 3:1–15 records a conversation that took place between Jesus and a Jewish Pharisee named Nicodemus. Nicodemus came to Jesus at night. He was—literally and spiritually—in the dark (3:2). During their nighttime conversation, Jesus told Nicodemus, "Unless one is born again he cannot see the kingdom of God" (3:3). Jesus explained the new birth to Nicodemus like this:

> Truly, truly, I say to you, unless one is born of water and the Spirit, he cannot enter

the kingdom of God. That which is born of the flesh is flesh, and that which is born of the Spirit is spirit. Do not marvel that I said to you, "You must be born again." The wind blows where it wishes, and you hear its sound, but you do not know where it comes from or where it goes. So it is with everyone who is born of the Spirit. (John 3:5–8)

Only those born of the Spirit can enter the kingdom of God. Why is spiritual birth necessary to be part of Christ's kingdom? Because in our natural condition, we are spiritually dead (Eph. 2:1–3). From the day of our biological birth, we are alienated from God and have no ability to please God or worship him rightly (Rom. 8:7–8). We need spiritual life. Jesus told Nicodemus that the Spirit of God gives life to spiritually dead sinners; they are "born of the Spirit."

What's the point? Local churches do not exist without Christians, and Christians would not exist apart from God's sovereign grace. He makes us alive, he gives us eyes to see and ears to hear the truth of the gospel. By God's grace, we are indwelt by his Spirit, confess Jesus as Lord (1 Cor. 12:3), and know truth from error (1 John 2:27).

Why is it so important that we understand what it means to be a Christian in our discussion of the local church? Well, let's return to the question I asked Lone Ranger at the beginning of this booklet. When Jesus says in Matthew 18:17, "Tell it to the church," who is that? Who is the church?

That's an important question because Jesus has given the local church a unique responsibility that no other earthly institution possesses. I'll explain what this responsibility is in the next section, but, simply put, Jesus has given local churches the authority to declare what is the true gospel and who is a true confessor of that gospel. That's an important job! Jesus wouldn't entrust that responsibility to just anyone. He gave that job to "the church" because the church is a group of Christians—born again, Spirit-indwelt people—who can distinguish the true gospel from a false one because they themselves have been born from above.

The kind of church Jesus has in mind in Matthew 18:17 is certainly not just the total number of people who show up to a building on Sunday morning. Sometimes our church has atheists, Mormons, or agnostics present in our Sunday morning gatherings. I am confident that Jesus did not give them the responsibility to address the brother in unrepentant sin. No, Jesus expects church *members* to address this brother because the church is a group of Christians who believe the gospel, agree on the gospel, are indwelt by the Spirit of Christ, and, as we will see in the next section, who assemble on earth as an embassy of Christ's heavenly kingdom.[2]

2. Who Assemble as an Earthly Embassy of Christ's Heavenly Kingdom

Assembly Day!

I can still remember my excitement in elementary school whenever our teacher told us that we were having an assembly. We called them "assembly days." I knew what that meant. It meant the whole school would gather in the gymnasium for a special event like a Christmas concert or a yo-yo demonstration—yes, I remember the yo-yo demonstration. I loved assembly days. Not only did we get out of class, but gathering with the whole student body was special. The rivalries between classes and grade levels faded. We all celebrated our unity as Lincoln Elementary School. We were all part of one student body—united by one common mascot (the lynx) and marked off by one common odor—you know, that stench that's unique to an elementary school cafeteria. Of all the experiences I had throughout my childhood education, the assemblies are still fresh in my mind and nose.

With even more enthusiasm than my second-grade self, I eagerly anticipate assembling with my church every week on the Lord's Day (Sunday). I get to gather with my church family to pray, to sing, to hear the word of God read and preached, and to partake of the ordinances. The Lord's Day assembly is a taste of heaven on earth.

A local church is an assembly. In fact, assembling together in one place at one time is essential to a church's churchiness. Just like a soccer team must assemble regularly for practices and games to exist as a team, a church must assemble regularly to be a church. It's part of what makes a church a church. In fact, the Greek word we translate as "church" is *ekklēsia*, and it means "assembly."[3]

Let's go back to Matthew 18:15–20 again. When Jesus taught his disciples how to handle a brother in unrepentant sin, he instructed them to bring this brother's sin before the *ekklēsia* (church), and if he refuses to listen to the *ekklēsia*, then the church should regard him as a Gentile and a tax collector (i.e., one who does not belong to Christ's kingdom; Matt. 18:17). Just a few verses later, Jesus said, "Where two or three are gathered in my name, there I am among them" (Matt. 18:20). Notice again what Jesus says here: "*Where* two or three are *gathered* in my name, *there* I am *among* them." The church (*ekklēsia*) in Matthew 18:17 is the assembly of two or three (or three hundred) gathered together in the same place. And *where* they are *gathered*, Jesus is *there*, meaning Jesus identifies with the assembly and authorizes the assembly to represent him so they can, among other things, make authoritative decisions about a brother in unrepentant sin.[4] It's common to hear people say a local church is a people not a place. But that statement isn't quite right. A church is a people assembled in a place.

Cold Fire, Square Circles, and Online Church

During the COVID-19 pandemic, many churches began holding online services. We now hear people talk about "online church." Some even think "online church" is a legitimate alternative to the way we typically "do church." But if the church is an assembly of two or three gathered in the same place, then how is a Zoom meeting or a virtual reality (VR) platform an assembly? To talk about online church is like talking about cold fire or square circles; "online church" is an unassembled assembly. It just doesn't work.

Some folks argue that virtual assemblies are still assemblies. We can, after all, still see each other, talk to each other, sing to each other, and hear the preaching of God's word through virtual platforms. Such reasoning, however, fails to recognize the fact that God has given us physical bodies and expects us to assemble, worship, and fellowship in geographical spaces in physical proximity—the "where" and "there" of the gathering (Matt. 18:20).

Imagine if you had to confine your relationship with your spouse to a virtual platform or give hugs to your children through your avatar! Those virtual relationships would be sub-human. Virtual reality is just that: virtual. Nobody gets a sunburn in VR; nobody dies in VR; nobody gets wet in the waters of baptism in VR. My brain might send panic signals to my body when my avatar stands on a tightrope between two skyscrapers, but if "I" fall, nobody needs to catch me.

Our bodies are an essential element of our humanity—you can't project them through digital media. Online church may sound innovative and evangelistic, but it inhibits discipleship, re-defines the local church, undermines our humanity, and cultivates consumerism (among other things). Jesus wants us to assemble so that we can administer a holy kiss (2 Cor. 13:12), a hearty handshake, or a slightly awkward side hug. No amount of technological advancement should keep Christians from assembling together as a church. They must assemble because Jesus commands it and because Jesus is there among them (Matt. 18:15–20).

Earthly Embassies of a Heavenly Kingdom

Two different assemblies meet at our church building. One meets every week on Sundays, the other meets every week on Mondays. Both are groups of Christians. Both groups teach the Bible. Both groups sing some songs together. Both have a statement of faith. Both have a leadership structure.

But one is a church, and one isn't.

The group that meets on Mondays is a classical education homeschool co-op. Parents and families gather every Monday to educate their children in a biblical worldview and to teach them to submit to Christ the King. Even though the homeschool cooperative is a group of Christians that gathers weekly, sings songs, affirms a statement of faith, and teaches biblical truth, it is not a church. Why? Because it's missing an essential mark: heaven's authority. The homeschool cooperative does not possess the authority to represent Christ's heavenly kingdom. Christ has not authorized Christian homeschool cooperatives to administer the ordinances, affirm people as citizens of Christ's kingdom, and expose false converts. He has given that kind of authority to local churches.

Think of it this way: local churches are like embassies. Embassies are institutions that represent the government of their home country on international soil. An embassy possesses the authority of the government it represents. A local church is like an embassy because Jesus has authorized local churches—two or three (or three hundred) gathered in Christ's name—to make authoritative decisions on earth on behalf of

Christ's heavenly kingdom. What kinds of decisions? They make decisions about what constitutes the true gospel and who makes a true confession of faith in that gospel.[5]

Let's return to Matthew's Gospel again. In Matthew 16:16, Peter made a bold proclamation about the identity of Jesus: "You are the Christ, the Son of the living God." Here's how Jesus responded to Peter's statement of faith:

> And Jesus answered him, "Blessed are you, Simon Bar-Jonah! For flesh and blood has not revealed this to you, but my Father who is in heaven. And I tell you, you are Peter, and on this rock I will build my church, and the gates of hell shall not prevail against it. I will give you the keys of the kingdom of heaven, and whatever you bind on earth shall be bound in heaven, and whatever you loose on earth shall be loosed in heaven." (Matt. 16:17–19)

Jesus not only affirmed the accuracy of Peter's gospel confession, he also entrusted Peter (and the apostles) with the keys of the kingdom of heaven. No, this doesn't mean that Peter is standing at the gate of heaven to determine who gets in and who doesn't. The keys of the kingdom of heaven gave Peter and the apostles the authority to do what Jesus just did: declare a true gospel confession from a false one and a true gospel confessor from a false one.

You might be wondering who wields the keys of heaven's kingdom now that the apostles are not around anymore. Did such authority vanish from the earth when the apostles died? No. Jesus gave the same authority to local churches. Let's return again to Matthew 18. This time, notice what Jesus says about the brother in unrepentant sin in Matthew 18:17–20:

> If he refuses to listen to them, tell it to the church. And if he refuses to listen even to the church, let him be to you as a Gentile and a tax collector. Truly, I say to you, whatever you bind on earth shall be bound in heaven, and whatever you loose on earth shall be loosed in heaven. Again I say to

you, if two of you agree on earth about anything they ask, it will be done for them by my Father in heaven. For where two or three are gathered in my name, there am I among them."

Matthew 18:17–20 does not mention the exact phrase, "keys of the kingdom of heaven," but it does repeat the language Matthew 16:19 uses to describe the function of the keys.

Matthew 16:19	Matthew 18:18
I will give you the keys of the kingdom of heaven, and whatever you bind on earth shall be bound in heaven, and whatever you loose on earth shall be loosed in heaven.	Truly, I say to you, whatever you bind on earth shall be bound in heaven, and whatever you loose on earth shall be loosed in heaven.

Jesus gave the church—two or three gathered in Christ's name—the authority to render decisions on earth on behalf of heaven. In Jesus's own words, "Whatever you bind on earth shall be bound in heaven, and whatever you loose on earth shall be loosed in heaven" (Matt. 18:18). The authority to bind and loose is the authority to make a judgment or render a verdict on earth on behalf of heaven.[6]

What does it look like practically for a local church to exercise the authority of the keys? Here are a few examples:

- Local churches guard the gospel by upholding the doctrinal content of their statement of faith.
- Local churches proclaim the gospel in their assemblies and herald the good news of Christ to the nations through missions and evangelism.
- Local churches administer baptism to new believers affirming them as citizens of Christ's heavenly kingdom.
- Local churches administer the Lord's Supper, celebrating each member's participation in Christ's new covenant family.

- Local churches excommunicate false converts, purifying the church and strengthening their witness of the gospel.

The local church is the only institution on earth entrusted with the responsibility of holding the keys of heaven. The homeschool cooperative may decide to admit a family into their program or remove a family from their school, but it does not have the authority to affirm whether or not someone is a citizen of Christ's heavenly kingdom. But my local church does. And so does every other local church scattered throughout the earth. They are earthly embassies of Christ's heavenly kingdom.

Churches often appear to the watching world as insignificant, weak, small, inconsequential organizations. My own church meets in a building that used to be a single-family home on a property once dedicated to raising horses. At one point, the youth ministry met in a renovated horse barn! Let's be honest, nobody drives by our little church building with its discolored bricks, undeveloped field of weeds, and unattractive youth barn and thinks to themselves, "Wow! That property is host to an embassy that represents the authority of the highest, most powerful, longest-lasting kingdom in the universe—the kingdom of heaven itself!" While people look at the Pentagon, the White House, and the US Capitol with a sense of awe, I'm sure many people look at our church building with a sense of pity.

But we shouldn't be surprised that God has entrusted seemingly insignificant assemblies of usually small numbers of Christians in often unimpressive buildings with the authority of heaven on earth. God chooses the weak things of the world to shame the strong (1 Cor. 1:27). Don't let the ordinariness of your own local church fool you into thinking it is insignificant. Your local church represents a heavenly kingdom that will last forever when all the kingdoms of men have faded away. When you assemble with your church, the geography of heaven comes to earth. And Jesus has entrusted you with a part in the responsibility to protect its sacred boundaries.

3. To Affirm One Another as His Citizens through the Ordinances

How do local churches affirm people as citizens of Christ's heavenly kingdom? Well, quite simply, through the ordinances of baptism and the Lord's Supper. Baptism and the Lord's Supper are like the passports of Christ's heavenly kingdom—they are badges of belonging. And who is authorized to administer these kingdom passports? Yep, you guessed it: the local church, the earthly embassy of Christ's heavenly kingdom.

Baptism

Baptism is a picture of conversion. It represents our death and resurrection with Christ. Symbolically, we go under to a watery grave and come out of those waters of death to walk in newness of life (Rom. 6:4). Picturing the beginning of the Christian life, baptism is how we publicly profess faith in Christ and identify ourselves with God and his people. We are baptized in the name of the Father, the Son, and the Holy Spirit

(Matt. 28:19). We bear God's name; we belong to his kingdom.

Baptism is like putting on a jersey to show what team we play for (Team Jesus), or a wedding ring to show that we are bound by covenant to a spouse (the church is the bride of Christ). Baptism is how local churches make outsiders insiders. That is, baptism brings people into the fellowship of the local church. The two or three gathered in Christ's name (Matt. 18:20) baptize four new believers in God's name (Matt. 28:19) to become six or seven gathered in Christ's name. The church grows through baptism, just as it did in Jerusalem when three thousand people were baptized and added to the church (Acts 2:41).

The Lord's Supper

Like baptism, the Lord's Supper is an ordinance Christ gave to his church. Unlike baptism, which in unique circumstances can happen independent of a local church—think frontier missions like Philip and the Ethiopian eunuch (Acts 8:26–40)—the Bible restricts the celebration of the

Lord's Supper to gatherings of the local church (1 Cor. 11:17–18, 20, 29, 33). Paul instructs us to "wait for one another" (1 Cor. 11:33) and to celebrate the Lord's Supper when we "come together as a church" (1 Cor. 11:18). In fact, celebrating the Lord's Supper is part of what makes a church a church. Paul says, "We who are many are one body, for [or *because*] we all partake of the one bread" (1 Cor. 10:17). Participation in the Lord's Supper turns individual Christians into one body, one church. If, as Bobby Jamieson has written, baptism "binds one to many," then the Lord's Supper "binds many into one."[7]

Baptism and the Lord's Supper together function as badges of belonging. They are kingdom passports. They mark out citizens of Christ's heavenly kingdom. In baptism, the church says to someone, "Hey, we think you're a Christian." At the Lord's Supper the church says to each member, "Hey, we still think each of you is a Christian!"

Together, baptism and the Lord's Supper give a local church its shape and its borders. They mark out who belongs to the church. Picture a local church as a brick building under construction. Each individual brick represents a baptized believer. The bricks get added one by one just as baptism adds new members one by one. Each individual brick is bound to the other bricks by mortar. All the bricks partake of the same mortar, cemented together into one beautiful brick building. The mortar is like the Lord's Supper because the Lord's Supper binds the individual Christians into one church. Without the mortar of the Lord's Supper, we would have no tangible, organized, and identifiable building. We would just have a pile of bricks scattered all over the yard. The bricks and the mortar give shape to the building just as baptism and the Lord's Supper give shape to the church.

4. To Proclaim the Good News and Commands of Christ the King

For a church to administer baptism and the Lord's Supper legitimately, it must first be a church that believes and proclaims the gospel.

Baptism and the Lord's Supper administered apart from the true gospel will get people wet and tickle their taste buds but nothing more. The ordinances will not function as passports of Christ's heavenly kingdom if the gospel is absent.

If you drive around in my city, you will find "churches" everywhere. But if you pay attention, you'll notice something peculiar. None of them have crosses. They are Mormon churches, part of the Church of Jesus Christ of Latter-Day Saints. Mormon churches are not true churches because they do not preach the biblical gospel. They preach another gospel—a gospel that is not good news and cannot save anyone from their sins (Gal. 1:6–9). You need more than a gathering of people in a building every Sunday to make a church. You need the gospel.

An essential mark of a true church is the right preaching of the gospel. No gospel, no church. After Peter confessed Jesus as the Christ, the Son of the living God, Jesus told Peter, "You are Peter, and on this rock I will build my church" (Matt. 16:18). The rock is Peter and his gospel confession. The rock is, in other words, the apostles and the gospel they preached. Jesus builds his church on the apostolic gospel. The church, wrote Paul, is "built on the foundation of the apostles and prophets, Christ Jesus himself being the cornerstone" (Eph. 2:20). God creates, builds, sustains, and nourishes his church through the gospel promised by the prophets in the Old Testament and made fully known by the apostles in the New Testament.

The book of Acts says that the early church "devoted themselves to the apostles' teaching" (Acts 2:42). When our local churches gather, we do the same thing. We open the Bible to read and hear what the apostles recorded about the life, ministry, and teachings of Jesus. We gather around the word of God to fulfill Jesus's command to make disciples of all nations, teaching them to observe all his commandments (Matt. 28:19–20).

The local church is where we learn what God accomplished in Jesus Christ at his cross and resurrection. It's where we learn how to respond to that gospel message with faith and repentance. It's where we learn what it means to be a disciple of Jesus. It's where we hear the gospel applied to our lives so that we can live in obedience to Christ our King. When a pastor preaches a sermon from the Bible, we collectively give our "yes" and "amen," testifying to the truth and authority of God's word. With the Spirit's help, the word of God causes the whole church to grow up into Christ as we mature in our discipleship and become more like Jesus our King (Eph. 4:11–16).

The risen Lord Jesus has entrusted no other earthly institution to proclaim, preserve, and protect the gospel. For two or three to gather *in Christ's name*, they must know Jesus Christ as he is revealed in the gospel. No gospel, no church.

5. To Display God's Own Holiness and Love through a Unified and Diverse People in All the World

Families, Airports, Lost Shoes, and the Local Church

I love walking through the airport with my family. People often stare at us. Usually they stare with smiles, but some people look shocked, a few even a little annoyed. Why? Because we have six children. Tromping through the airport with six young kids tends to grab people's attention.

Families are beautiful. Some people will even compliment me on my family. "Your children are so sweet and so well-behaved," they say. I always smile and thank them while secretly hoping these people don't end up sitting in front of my three-year-old on the flight. My family is beautiful.

And, yet, like every family, we have our struggles. We experience trials, tears, discipline issues, conflicts, forgiveness, a love-hate relationship with car seats, mealtimes around the kitchen table, shoes that magically disappear when we need them most, birthday celebrations, and love that binds us together—except when someone loses a shoe. Yet through it all, we're a family. We bear the same name; we live in the same house; we sacrifice for each other; we love each other. The bonds of fatherhood, motherhood, brotherhood, and sisterhood bind us together.

The New Testament describes the church in many ways—a temple, a royal priesthood, a

holy nation, a bride, and a city, among others
(Eph. 2:20–22; 5:22–33; 1 Pet. 2:9; Rev. 21:2).
The New Testament also presents the church as a
family. The church, said Paul, is the "household
of God" (Eph. 2:19; 1 Tim. 3:15) made up of
God's children. As Christians, God has adopted
us as sons and filled us with the Spirit of his Son
by whom we cry, "Abba! Father!" (Rom. 8:15).
The church is a family bound together by bonds
more enduring than biological bloodlines.

As God's family, indwelt by God's Spirit, our
churches should reflect God's holiness and God's
love. Remember, the church is not a man-made
invention; it's God's creation. Born-again believers have new desires and new affections. No lon-
ger enslaved by the passions of the flesh, we desire
to honor God and to love God's people from a
pure heart (1 Pet. 1:22–23). Or as Jesus said, "By
this all people will know that you are my disciples,
if you have love for one another" (John 13:35).

It makes perfect sense when people unite
over a common interest like political parties,
country club amenities, cultural customs, or
Chuck Norris movies. But God has made a

loving family—indeed a new humanity—out of people from different backgrounds, different ethnicities, different ages, different cultures, different interests, and different convictions. Jesus calls Jews and Gentiles, prostitutes and Pharisees, tax-collectors and anti-Roman zealots, home-school moms and hardcore rockers to become part of his church. When we gather with our local churches as a loving and unified yet diverse people, the world takes notice. "All people will know you are my disciples"—that's how Jesus put it (John 13:35).

Love's Discipline

For a church to display God's holiness and love, it must practice church discipline. In fact, church discipline is an essential mark of a local church. It is also an essential part of showing love. Do you remember how Jesus identified the man in unrepentant sin in Matthew 18:15–20? He referred to him as "your brother" (Matt. 18:15). If a brother in sin refuses to repent, we are to bring his sin before the whole family (the church) to discipline him. If the family loves this "brother," they will discipline him for his good. They will warn him, tell him the truth, call him to repentance, and even excommunicate him in hopes that he will repent. Church discipline takes God's holiness seriously; it takes love seriously (1 Cor. 5:1–13).

Maybe you think church discipline sounds unloving and harsh. But love without discipline is like swimming without water—it's not really swimming; it's not really love. The author of Hebrews reminded his readers that God disciplines those he loves, just as earthly fathers discipline their own children because they love them (Heb. 12:3–11). No discipline, no love.

Gerald knows the benefit of love's discipline.[8] Gerald was a member of our church for several years, but after becoming close with some Mormon friends, he decided to get baptized into the Mormon church. Our hearts were broken, but we didn't give up on Gerald because we loved him. When Gerald had become a member of our church, we made a covenant with him to faithfully warn, rebuke, and admonish him if necessary.

Seeking to love Gerald and follow Jesus, we started to walk through the process of Matthew 18. One brother confronted him. When he wouldn't turn from his sin, that brother took another two brothers as witnesses to confront him again (Matt. 18:16). Still, Gerald refused to turn from his sin. But we intended to keep our covenant promises to Gerald, so we informed the whole church of his situation and began to pray for Gerald's soul. We prayed that he would repent. The whole congregation pursued Gerald and pointed him back to the Bible. We told him he was wrong because we loved him. We warned him that in a short time, our church would discipline him unless he repented because we loved him. We rebuked him because we loved him.

After many conversations, Gerald repented! He came back to our church, renounced Mormonism, and reaffirmed his belief in the true gospel. Gerald remains a faithful Christian today. God used the local church to shower Gerald with love's discipline, the kind of love that cares about God's holiness and Gerald's eternal happiness.

6. Following the Teaching and Example of the Elders

I once purchased a piece of furniture from a young man in a nearby city. While we carried the heavy object to my car, he asked me a question: "What do you do for work?"

"I'm a pastor," I said.

"Oh, so you do shows and stuff like that?" he responded.

I was caught off-guard. Shows? Did he mean like theatrical plays? TV shows? Puppet shows? This young man clearly had no idea what a pastor is and what a pastor does. I tried to explain to him what it means to be a pastor on our short walk together. I don't think he was impressed as I told him that I teach the Bible, pray for people, try to love and care for them, and show them with my life how to be a disciple of Jesus. But that's what pastors do.

Local churches are led by pastors. The New Testament actually uses three different words to describe the office of the pastor: "overseer" (1 Tim. 3:1), "elder" (1 Pet. 5:1), and pastor (Eph.

4:11). Each word refers to the same office of leadership in a local church. Pastors are elders, elders are pastors, overseers are elders, and so forth.

Elders lead churches. Granted, churches can exist without elders. The two or three gathered in Christ's name administering the ordinances is a church even without any elders. But healthy churches will strive to have a plurality of qualified elders leading the church (1 Tim. 3:1–7). A local church without a pastor is still a church, but that church will be like a classroom without a teacher, a team without a coach, a flock of sheep without a shepherd.

Faithful elders are Christ's gift to local churches (Eph. 4:8–11). They are men of exemplary character and capable of teaching sound doctrine (1 Tim. 3:1–7). They model Christian maturity (1 Tim. 4:12–13), pray for the saints (James 5:13–15), and equip the saints for the work of the ministry (Eph. 4:11–12). Faithful pastors will use their authority to teach their church members how to exercise their congregational authority wisely. Remember, it's the two or three gathered—the congregation—that wields the keys of the kingdom together. Church members should submit to the elders and learn from them so that they can better fulfill their responsibilities to guard the gospel, evangelize the lost, disciple others, and love their brothers and sisters.

It's hard to overstate the importance of the role of faithful pastors in the local church. God has given churches shepherds who keep watch over our souls as those who will give an account (Heb. 13:17). I'm thankful for the doctors that help me with physical problems. I am beyond grateful for faithful pastors—physicians of the soul—that pray for me, encourage me from God's word, warn me if I stray, and do everything in their power to ensure that I arrive at the heavenly city when my earthly life is complete. You would do well to pray for your pastors and encourage them often. They are God's gift to you.

To Him Be Glory in the Church

Will you have an answer next time someone asks you, "What is a church anyway?" I hope so.

Despite all the flaws you have probably seen in your own local church (every church has them), I hope this booklet has helped you understand the importance of the local church and encouraged you to spend your life serving Christ's church until he returns or calls you home. Jesus has given us work to do together that we cannot do by ourselves. Jesus loves the church. He loves the local church. I hope you do too.

My hunch is that most Christians love their churches but underestimate its significance. The local church is not an optional bonus to the Christian life. It's not merely a perk we enjoy as citizens of Christ's kingdom. The local church is essential; it stands at the center of God's redemptive activity in the world. The church is an embassy of a coming heavenly kingdom— a foretaste of future glory. Next time you gather with your church around the word of God to pray, to sing, and to partake of the bread and the cup, remember that your ordinary assembly testifies to God's extraordinary work of redemption that will culminate in the new heavens and new earth. When you gather with your church, you are a people of the future—part of a new humanity that will inherit an eternal kingdom when Christ comes again. As often as we eat the bread and drink the cup, we proclaim the Lord's death *until he comes* (1 Cor. 11:26).

One day, heaven will come to earth. Until then, lone-ranger Christianity is not Jesus's plan for his disciples—it never will be. We assemble now anticipating our future assembly at the marriage supper of the Lamb (Rev. 19:6–10).

The Westminster Catechism famously asks, "What is the chief end of man?" to which it rightly answers, "To glorify God and enjoy him forever." But twentieth-century Australian minister David Broughton Knox certainly had biblical warrant when he proposed a slight revision: "What is the chief end of man? To glorify God and enjoy him *in the company of his people* forever."[9]

> To him be glory in the church and in Christ Jesus throughout all generations, forever and ever. Amen. (Eph. 3:21)

Notes

1. Collin Hansen and Jonathan Leeman, *Rediscover Church: Why the Body of Christ Is Essential* (Wheaton, IL: Crossway, 2021), 26. I have altered the order of some of their phrases, but the language is theirs.
2. If you want more information on church membership, see Jonathan Leeman, *Church Membership: How the World Knows Who Represents Jesus* (Wheaton, IL: Crossway, 2012).
3. See Jonathan Leeman, *One Assembly: Rethinking the Multisite and Multiservice Church Models* (Wheaton, IL: Crossway, 2020), 41–98.
4. Leeman, *One Assembly*, 58–59.
5. Jonathan Leeman, *Don't Fire Your Church Members: The Case for Congregationalism* (Nashville, TN: B&H Academic, 2016), 74–81.
6. Leeman, *Don't Fire Your Church Members*, 77.
7. Bobby Jamieson, *Going Public: Why Baptism Is Required for Church Membership* (Nashville: B&H Academic, 2015), 122.

8. This story is shared with permission, and names have been changed for privacy.
9. David Broughton Knox, quoted in Mark Thompson, "Knox/Robinson for Today (Extended)," The Briefing, Dec. 20, 2011, http://thebriefing.com.au.

Scripture Index

IX 9Marks

Building Healthy Churches

9Marks exists to equip church leaders with
a biblical vision and practical resources
for displaying God's glory to the nations
through healthy churches.

To that end, we want to see churches
characterized by these nine marks
of health:

1. Expositional Preaching
2. Gospel Doctrine
3. A Biblical Understanding of
   Conversion and Evangelism
4. Biblical Church Membership
5. Biblical Church Discipline
6. A Biblical Concern for
   Discipleship and Growth
7. Biblical Church Leadership
8. A Biblical Understanding
   of the Practice of Prayer
9. A Biblical Understanding and
   Practice of Missions

Find all our Crossway titles
and other resources at
9Marks.org.

IX 9Marks Church Questions

Providing ordinary Christians with sound and accessible biblical teaching by answering common questions about church life.

For more information, visit crossway.org.